365 Things Every Golfer Should Know

DOUG FIELDS

HARVEST HOUSE PUBLISHERS
Eugene, Oregon 97402

Cover by Terry Dugan Design, Minneapolis, Minnesota

365 THINGS EVERY GOLFER SHOULD KNOW
Copyright © 2002 by Doug Fields
Published by Harvest House Publishers
Eugene, Oregon 97402

ISBN 0-7369-0921-4

Published in association with the literary agency of *Alive Communications, Inc.,* 7680 Goddard Street, Suite 200, Colorado Springs CO 80920.

Printed in the United States of America.

05 06 07 08 09 10 / BC-MS / 10 9

Contents

To Jim Fields

I wish you could still play golf, Dad! Thanks for teaching me everything I know and for being excited the first time I ever beat you...I'll never forget that. In heaven you won't be crippled with Parkinson's disease, and who knows— maybe we can play a few rounds together.

———

Thanks to Kurt Johnston, Matt Hall, Steve Rutenbar, and Cody Fields (my favorite foursome) for helping with these ideas, straightening my slice, and turning your heads when it's time for another mulligan.

1

Quotes
and Quips

Golf is one of those games
where nobody else can
take credit for your
ability...or wants to.

—UNKNOWN

———

Nobody ever looked up
and saw a good shot.

—DON HEROLD

Actually, the Lord answers
my prayers everywhere
except on the golf course.

—Billy Graham

———

Half of golf is fun;
the other half is putting.

—Peter Dobereiner

By the time a man can
afford to lose a golf ball,
he can't hit it that far.

—Lewis Grizzard

———

Gimme: an agreement
between two losers
who can't putt.

—John Bishop

Golf is a game in which
you yell "fore," shoot six,
and write down five.

—PAUL HARVEY

———

I have a tip that can
take five strokes off
anyone's golf game.
It's called an eraser.

—ARNOLD PALMER

11

I think I fail just a bit less
than everyone else.

—BYRON NELSON

———

As you walk down
the fairway of life you
must smell the roses,
for you only get to
play one round.

—BEN HOGAN

If you watch a game, it's fun. If you play it, it's recreation. If you work at it, it's golf

—BOB HOPE

———

I'm not saying my golf game went bad, but if I grew tomatoes they would have come up sliced.

—LEE TREVINO

It took me 17 years
to get 3000 hits in baseball.
I did it in one afternoon
on the golf course.

—HANK AARON

Forgetting what lies
behind, I push on.

—THE APOSTLE PAUL

When you play the game
for fun, it's fun. When you
play it for a living, it's a
game of sorrows.

—GARY PLAYER

————

You can talk to a fade,
but a hook won't listen.

—LEE TREVINO

I can air mail the
golf ball a long distance,
but sometimes I don't put
the right address on it.

—JIM DENT

———

Golf and women are
a lot alike. You know you
are not going to end up
with anything but grief, but
you can't resist the impulse.

—JACKIE GLEASON

When Jack Nicklaus plays
well, he wins. When he
plays badly, he comes in
second. When he plays ter-
ribly, he comes in third.

—Johnny Miller

———

I don't think TV has
messed up my game.
I've pretty much taken
care of that on my own.

—Curtis Strange

The older I get,
the better I used to be.

—LEE TREVINO

———

My biggest fear
is having to go out
and get a real job.

—FUZZY ZOELLER

18

Every hole should
be a hard par and
an easy bogey.

—ROBERT TRENT JONES

———

Three things I fear:
lightning, Ben Hogan,
and a downhill putt.

—SAM SNEAD

2

Goofy Golf
Definitions

Practice Tee:
A place where golfers go
to convert a nasty hook
into a wicked slice

———

Mulligan:
Invented by an Irishman
who wanted to hit one
more 20-yard grounder

Oxymoron:
An easy par three

———

Bob Barker:
A shot that's hit
so high that you want
it to "come on down"

Cart Path:
A hard, smooth surface
that can add 30 yards
to your drive.

———

Golf:
A five-mile walk
punctuated with
disappointments

3

Interesting
Facts

The first professional
golf tournament was held
in 1860. The prize—a red
leather belt.

———

The first instructional
book about golf
was written
in 1687.

The Hershey Chocolate
Company was the first
corporate sponsor
of a golf tournament.

———

The first televised golf
tournament aired in 1947.

The first 18-hole course in
America was built in 1892.

———

Graphite shafts were
introduced in 1973.

Metal woods were
introduced in 1979
by Taylor Made.

———

More than 26 million
Americans play golf.

Approximately 90 percent of golfers shoot in the 100s.

———

The longest recorded hole-in-one was 447 yards, hit on October 7, 1965.

There are more
sesame seeds on a Big Mac
than there are dimples
on a golf ball.

————

Callaway is the world's
largest golf company.

The average drive
leaves the tee at
160 miles per hour.

———

The maximum weight for a
golf ball is 1.62 ounces.

The highest recorded score
on a par three is 166.

———

Pine Valley golf course
in New Jersey has the
largest bunker in the world.
It's one-half acre.

Americans spend
more than $630 million
a year on golf balls.

———

There are more than
10,000 golf courses
in the U.S.

The only person to
play golf on the moon
was Alan Shepard.

———

The United States Golf
Association (USGA) was
founded in 1894 as the
governing body of golf in
the United States.

Before 1850, golf balls were
made of leather and were
stuffed with feathers.

———

4

The Rule
Book and the
Bible

Patience is better than pride (Ecclesiastes 7:8).

———

A wise man controls his temper. He knows that anger causes mistakes (Proverbs 14:29).

A relaxed attitude
lengthens a man's life
(Proverbs 14:30).

———

You may carry no more
than 14 clubs in your bag.

You aren't allowed to
take a practice swing
in a sand trap.

———

You can't tee the ball up
on the fairway.

40

The three basic rules:

(a) Play the course as you find it.
(b) Play the ball as it lies.
(c) If you can't do either of these, do what's fair.

———

It is legal to putt out of a bunker (but don't try it).

5

Fun Golf Terms from A to Z

Alligator putt:
A putt with a lot of bumps
along the way

———

Bass bait:
A ball hit into deep water

Candles:
Scoring eleven on a hole

———

Direct deposit:
A hole in one

Easter egg:
A found ball
(not your own)

———

Fly paper:
Slow greens

Gut truck:
Beverage cart

———

Home run:
Hitting a shot
out-of-bounds and
over a fence

In jail:
An impossible lie—
there's no way out!

———

Jailer:
An impolite golfer
who rattles his keys
while you're putting

Knee knocker:
A drive that is
only knee high

———

Loaf:
A huge divot stuck
on your club

Military golf:
Hitting the ball left, left,
left, right, left

———

Nails:
A pair of golf shoes

Out house:
Making par with
an out-of-bounds

———

PISO:
Phooey, I'm still out

Quack:
A sharp hook

———

Rabbit:
A putt that hops along
into the hole

Scuba diving:
Scooping the ball out of
the water with your club

———

Tigered it:
Reached a par five
in two strokes

UBE:
Ugly But Effective

Victory lap:
A ball that lips the hole
before going in

Water wedge:
Ball retriever

———

Xeroxers:
Copy or knock-off clubs

Yips:
Uncontrollable nervousness
before putting

———

Zorro:
Scoring a par without ever
being in the fairway

6

Never on a
Golf Course

Never walk in another
player's putting line.

———

Never enter a bunker
from the front.

Never bring your clubs
onto the green.

———

Never be late
for your tee time.

Never hit into the
group ahead of you.
Let the marshal
keep play moving.

———

Never talk or make noise
when someone is putting
or addressing the ball.

Never leave a ball mark
on the green unrepaired.

———

Never bring a cell phone
to the course.

Never play golf
during an electrical storm.
Ask Lee Trevino.

———

Never go to the tee
without a spare ball
in your pocket.

Never play a mulligan
with a group waiting
behind you.

————

Never continue playing out
a hole when you've reached
triple bogey. Pick up.

Never write down your
score while on the green
you've just completed.
Move ahead.

———

Never turn in a score that
isn't the truth. You're only
cheating yourself.

7

Exercises in
Etiquette

Know your favorite course's
tee-time policies.

———

Always have a few good,
clean golf jokes.

If you've been looking
for five minutes and
can't find your ball,
let it rest in peace.

———

When on the green, put
your mark behind the ball.

Amateurs shouldn't
wear knickers.

———

At home, refrain
from using your putter
as a hammer.

When on the range,
don't cheer when
someone hits the guy
picking up the balls.

———

Don't ever volunteer
to be the range ball guy.

Striped balls belong
only on the range.

———

When your start time is in
the morning, bring a fresh
donut for the starter.

Don't golf without
your spouse on your
honeymoon.

———

Golf equipment doesn't
qualify as a romantic gift.

Your son or daughter
probably doesn't want
to hear about your
approach on fifteen.

———

Make a high handicapper
feel good by asking for a
piece of advice.

Be sure to stand *behind*
the person hitting.

———

Let someone else drive the
cart for a change.

No one likes a bragger.

———

Stop and enjoy the
scenery—just don't stop
for too long.

Throwing grass
in the air before you shoot
makes you look cool.

———

Throwing grass
in the air and having it
blow back in your face
makes you look foolish.

When your friend asks
to borrow a ball, give him
an orange one.

———

It's unsafe to
throw your clubs.

"Sorry to hear about your last stroke" has more than one meaning when playing with your grandfather.

———

Be nice to the course marshal.

The foot wedge
is an illegal club.

———

You aren't expected to
know the entire rule book.

The person who talks the
most about the rules is
probably the one who
cheats the most.

———

The statute of limitations
on forgotten strokes
is two holes.

Bets lengthen putts
and shorten drives.

———

Never wash your ball on
the tee of a water hole.

Make sure you're
enjoyable to play with.

———

Giving an extra mulligan
is good for the heart.

Watch your language.

———

Fore is an acceptable
four-letter word.

"Nice lag" really
means "lousy putt."

———

Always concede
the fourth putt.

Give advice to a
struggling player.

———

Accept advice gracefully.

Don't leave etiquette
on the course—take it
everywhere you go.

———

Discover the power of
well-timed encouragement.

Be a good winner.

———

Call ahead to find out
what the dress code is.

Learn how to politely
decline a wager.

———

Make the greens
keeper smile.

Know when to give
advice and when to keep
your mouth shut.

———

If you're away,
you're first to play.

Always repair
your ball mark.

———

Always replace your divot.

Never set your
bag on the green.

————

When tending the flag,
don't leave your shadow
over the hole
or the putter's line.

Never step on someone's
putting line.

———

Rake the sand trap.

Keep up with the group
in front of you.

———

Let faster groups
play through.

Be ready to play
when it's your turn.

———

Wait until you reach
the next tee box
to record your score.

Most courses
require soft spikes.

———

Try not to hit anyone.

Don't lose your temper;
it's just a game.

———

Give your boss a mulligan.

Leave the trash talking
to basketball players.

———

8

Words to the
Wise

Golf should be
a relaxing sport.

———

Golf can be stressful.

Remember the phrase
"drive for show,
putt for dough."

———

Never wear plaid.

Stroke the ball, don't hit it.

———

Keep your head down.

Always take
a practice swing.

———

Don't take a practice swing
in the pro shop.

An ideal round of golf
should take four hours.

———

Your backswing should
take twice as long
as your downswing.

Always use a
pre-shot routine.

———

Always use a
post-shot excuse.

It's not the club,
it's the clubber.

———

When your ball is near
the fringe, make the putter
your first club choice.

If your ball lies
on a hill above your feet,
choke up a little.

———

Stretch yourself…play
a challenging course
every now and then.

Your tee is a great tool
for cleaning the grooves
in your clubs.

———

Don't let an impatient
golfer behind you
ruin your round.

Carry a golf towel…
it's useful when you
miss that two-foot
putt—for tears.

———

Water is the
best sport drink.

Buy a windbreaker.

———

Don't buy the $120 pro shop windbreaker.

Learn to hit
with distractions.

———

Videotape your swing
a few times a year.

Wear sunglasses
whenever possible.

———

Most courses have the
yardage marked on the
fairway sprinkler heads.

Short and straight is better
than long and crooked.

———

Go to a pro tournament at
least once in your lifetime.

Drink plenty of water
in hot weather.

———

The quality of practice
is more important
than the quantity.

Don't let a bad game
turn into a bad day.

———

That whole "be the ball"
thing doesn't work.

Don't park by
the driving range.

———

Short holes are never as
short as you think.

Learn how to play
a four-man scramble.

———

Keep sunscreen
in your bag.

Enjoy yourself.

———

If you really want to be
better at golf, go back
and take it up at
a much earlier age.

No golfer ever
swung too slowly.

———

No golfer ever
played too fast.

Never keep more than 300 separate thoughts in your mind during your swing.

———

When your shot has to carry over a water hazard, you can either hit one more club or two more balls.

Know how far you hit
the ball with each club.

———

Know how far the next rest
room is before passing one.

Boost your confidence
by playing miniature golf
every now and then…with
your kids.

———

If you can't play well, at
least dress like you can.

For better traction, keep
your spikes clean.

—

The best days to golf are
those that end in "y."

Don't believe the myths;
there's no need
for stamina in golf.

———

Make sure you eat
before you play—for
better stamina.

When in a waiting room,
read the golf
magazines first.

———

The secret of good golf
is to hit the ball hard,
straight, and not too often.

Laugh when you
feel like crying.

———

Say no to golf once in a
while and yes to four hours
with your family instead.

Memorize a few very
obscure golf rules.

Learn to make a whiff
look like a practice swing.

Lessons are
worth the money.

———

Lessons aren't
always the answer.

Don't use striped tube
socks as head covers.

———

Always have a good excuse
ready for a bad shot.
("These new shoes are
killing my stance.")

Keep your sense of humor.

———

Do not give lessons
to your spouse.

Don't lose your joy.

———

Most scoring occurs within
100 yards of the hole.

Putting is 68 percent
of the game.

———

Learn how to calculate
a handicap.

Don't think about the
water…the water…
the water (plunk).

———

Know when to lay up.

It might be wise to buy
your spouse a new "some-
thing" instead of buying
yourself a new driver.

———

Children don't want
to watch golf on TV
with you.

The best putter
usually wins.

———

Train your swing,
then trust it.

Form a loose grip.

———

Use the wind,
don't fight it.

A ball sitting in a divot
will come out lower
and roll longer.

———

A ball sitting in the trap
tends to stay there
for a few strokes.

Stretch.

———

If you can putt the ball,
do so.

Keep the ball
low in the wind.

———

Use more club
on an uphill lie.

Don't waste your money
on silly golf gadgets.

———

Practice your short game
twice as much
as your drive.

Revisit a couple of
golf's greatest moments.

———

Familiarize yourself
with some legends
from the PGA:

SNEAD, JONES, NICKLAUS,
HOGAN, PALMER, NELSON, CASPER,
HAGEN, AND MIDDLECOFF.

Follow some of the key tournaments:

THE MASTERS, THE PGA CHAMPIONSHIP, THE U.S. OPEN, THE BRITISH OPEN, THE RYDER CUP, AND THE SKINS GAME.

Learn about some of the world's greatest courses:

PEBBLE BEACH, AUGUSTA, ST. ANDREWS, ROYAL TROON, TPC AT SAWGRASS, WINGED FOOT, PINE VALLEY, CYPRESS POINT, SHINNECOCK, PINEHURST, MERION, VALDERRAMA, OLYMPIC, AND RIVIERA.

9

Some Self-Made
Thoughts

The ball will almost always break away from hills and toward water.

———

The ball almost always breaks away from the cup.

The faults in your swing
can never be cured
in just one lesson
from a professional.

———

A dime makes
a good ball mark.

It's bad when your divot
goes farther than your ball.

———

It's bad when your divot
is larger than your toupee.

White golf gloves
never seem to last
as long as black ones.

———

Golf carts don't float.

Learn how to use
a tee as a toothpick.

———

It's impossible to look
cool in saddle shoes.

When you're on the tee,
imagine a gallery full
of people on each side
of the fairway.

———

When you're on the tee,
imagine all the people
lining the fairway are
injury attorneys.

Stop thinking about
results you don't want.

———

Most of golf is played
"between the ears."

If it goes right, it's a slice.
If it goes left, it's a hook.
If it goes straight,
it's a miracle.

———

Curly, downhill, left-to-
right putts are usually
followed by curly, uphill,
right-to-left putts.

Delicate chip shots
over bunkers always catch
the top of the bank
and fall back.

————

Golf is a lot like life—
the sooner you get over
your mistakes, the better
off you'll be.

Never carry an umbrella
in your bag; if it's raining
that hard you shouldn't
be out there anyway.

———

If you have to yell
fore more than twice
in a round, it's time
to go home.

A three-foot putt can
be much tougher than
a forty-footer.

———

It's better to laugh at
yourself than to get
angry at yourself.

In life, there are
no gimmes.

———

Golf is still
a gentleman's game.

Pull carts aren't cool...
unless you're in your 70s.

———

Walking is more
enjoyable than riding.

Golf is a simple game.

———

Golf is the hardest
game in the world.

Even professionals
have "first tee jitters."

———

The game lies
in the journey.

A bad day on a golf course
is better than a good day
in a bowling alley.

———

Golf is a game
of mistake management.

God doesn't care
how well you putt.

————

Integrity counts—on
and off the course.

High-priced golf balls
won't help your score.

———

Old balls seldom
get lost.

It's only a game.

———

Your best shot of the day
will be the one
nobody sees.

Golf infomercials
exaggerate.

———

It's okay to play
from the white tees.

Taking a child to
the driving range is fun.

———

You're usually the safest
when standing in the
middle of the fairway.

Learn how to spot
a collectible club at a
garage sale or thrift shop.

———

Golf carts always break
down at the farthest point
from the clubhouse.

No matter how bad your
last shot was, the worst
is yet to come.

———

Your best round of golf
will be followed almost
immediately by your
worst round ever.

Trees are 90% air...
but you'll always hit
the other 10%.

———

Golf balls rarely bounce off
trees and back into play.

Brand new golf balls
are water-magnetic.

———

All three woods
are demon-possessed.

Golf was once a rich man's sport, but now it has millions of poor players.

——

An amateur golfer is one who addresses the ball twice: once before swinging, and once again after swinging.

Thank God for
the ability to swing a club.

———

You will be tempted to
cheat every time you play.

You cannot master
this game.

———

Remember,
God is watching.

If you've stopped smiling,
it might be time
to stop playing.

———

Golf is the best game in
the world to be bad at.

Golf is the only game
where the better you are,
the less you play.

———

There actually is a sweet
spot on every club.

Hazards attract
and fairways repel.

———

Golf is harder than
baseball because in golf
your foul balls count.

Golfers who try to make
everything perfect before
taking the shot rarely make
the perfect shot.

———

The term "mulligan" is
really a contraction of the
phrase "maul-it-again."

It takes 17 holes
to get warmed-up.

———

One birdie is a hot streak.

The rake is always
in the other trap.

———

The less skilled the player,
the more likely he is
to share his ideas about
the golf swing.

It's surprisingly easy
to hole a 50-foot putt
when you lie 10.

———

When someone says,
"Uh…I think I got a five,"
or "Why don't you give
me a five?" he really means
he got a seven.

The wind is usually in your
face on 16 of the 18 holes.

———

The rough will
be mowed tomorrow.

It never begins to rain
on the eighteenth hole.

———

It always takes at least
four holes to notice
that a club is missing.

The ball always
lands where the pin
was yesterday.

———

The practice green is either
half as fast or twice as fast
as all the other greens.

No one with silly head
covers ever broke par.

———

If you're hitting your shots
straight on the driving
range, it's probably
because you're not
aiming at anything.

Golf is proof that God
has a sense of humor.

———

God will bring you
through every trial
and tribulation.

It's time to give up
the game when you're
spending more time in
the sand than a lifeguard.

———

The shorter the putt,
the smaller the hole
becomes.

The shortest distance
between the ball and
the target is never
a straight line.

———

Looking up the rule
always works against you.

The three worst words to hear are "You're still away."

———

What is printed on a golf ball is not a guarantee. Example: "long distance."

It doesn't matter how far
you hit the ball if you
don't hit it straight.

———

Learn how to pray.

Attitude is more
important than ability.

———

Don't be afraid
to dream a little.

Approach your shot
with confidence.

———

Confidence evaporates
in the presence of water.

The condition of your
heart is more important
than the condition
of your swing.

———

Golf tends to make you
believe in the doctrine
of predestination.

You are more likely to be
struck by lightning on a
golf course than bitten by a
shark in the ocean.

———

A dogleg isn't
man's best friend.

A long day on the course
will cause you to eat food
from a snack bar that
you wouldn't normally
give to your dog.

———

Living below par is
only acceptable on
the golf course.

You *can* hit the broad
side of a barn.

——

If there is a leaf on
the course, your ball is
probably under it.

The driving range
is a hilarious first date.

———

Golf pros make everything
look easier than it is.

For less than the cost
of a round of golf, you can
support a needy child through
Compassion International
for several months
(www.compassion.com).

—————

Most people who don't like
golf have never played it.

Church is still
the best place to spend
a Sunday morning.

———

There is someone out
there worse than you.

Buy used clubs and donate
the financial difference
to a charity.

———

Alice Cooper plays golf
every day.

A round of golf can be
a great Mother's Day
or Father's Day gift.

———

A sleeve of golf balls makes
a great stocking stuffer.

A round of golf can
be a great four-hour
conversation with
an old friend.

———

Golf can be a great
opportunity to meet
a new friend.

It's never too late
to pick up the game.

———

It's okay to be a hacker.

It's easier said than done.

———

Clean your ball
between holes.

Not all fairways are fair.

———

Not all greens are green.

If it was easy to hit out of,
it wouldn't be called
the "rough."

———

Other Good Harvest House Reading

365 Things Every Couple Should Know
By Doug Fields
"Don't yell at each other unless the house is on fire" is one of the witty sayings that encourage couples to demonstrate greater love for one another and experience more romance and fun together.

100 Fun and Fabulous Ways to Flirt with Your Spouse
By Doug Fields, artwork by Marian Nixon
100 clever ideas, from foot massages to love notes and heart-shaped pancakes, make it easy for couples celebrating a marriage or anniversary to ignite the spark of romance with flirtatious fun throughout the years.